HEAVEN AND BACK!

DAWN KELLY

D1641702

Heaven and Back

Trilogy Christian Publishers
A Wholly Owned Subsidiary of Trinity Broadcasting Network
2442 Michelle Drive
Tustin, CA 92780

Copyright © 2020 by Dawn Kelly

All Scripture quotations, unless otherwise noted, taken from THE HOLY BIBLE, NEW INTERNATIONAL VERSION®, NIV® Copyright © 1973, 1978, 1984, 2011 by Biblica, Inc.® Used by permission. All rights reserved worldwide.

All rights reserved, including the right to reproduce this book or portions thereof in any form whatsoever.
For information, address Trilogy Christian Publishing
Rights Department, 2442 Michelle Drive, Tustin, Ca 92780.
Trilogy Christian Publishing/ TBN and colophon are trademarks of Trinity Broadcasting Network.
For information about special discounts for bulk purchases, please contact Trilogy Christian Publishing.
Manufactured in the United States of America

Trilogy Disclaimer: The views and content expressed in this book are those of the author and may not necessarily reflect the views and doctrine of Trilogy Christian Publishing or the Trinity Broadcasting Network.

10 9 8 7 6 5 4 3 2 1
Library of Congress Cataloging-in-Publication Data is available.
ISBN 978-1-64773-690-3
E-ISBN 978-1-64773-691-0

A New Journey

When you have gone through what I have been through, you really do not know where to begin. I was always a sick child. I thought it was normal. Six months before my health had major issues, the Lord told me that I was going to be ill, but he was going to bring me through. I said, "Okay Lord, I can handle this. I can go through whatever it is because I trust you." I knew that it would push me into a divine destiny. I had no idea what God was about to do in my life.

It started in July 2015. I started experiencing acid reflux, vomiting, and severe stomach pain. It went on for three days. During the three days, I tried to see my primary care physician, but the earliest appointment was not until the following week.

By that time, I felt better, but I went to the appointment anyway. There were numerous of scans done. I had chronic pancreatitis before, so they were trying to rule out that I did not have it again. That was ruled out. What they did find was that I had pancreatic cysts. So, they arranged for me to see a Gastrologist. I went to see the specialist for more tests. Those tests lead me to having an endoscopic out-patient procedure. My family and some dear sisters in Christ came to support me. I kept saying to myself, this is a piece of cake. God has me. I can do this.

During the procedure, while I was still under anesthesia, the doctor came out to tell my family that I had pancreatic cancer. He said it was spreading to my liver, and it was spreading fast. The doctor also told them that he could not do surgery because of the aggression of the cancer. He recommended that I should begin chemotherapy and radiation immediately. What I forgot to mention was the Thursday prior to the procedure, the Lord had given me word for the praise team. The word was "Will you worship me when the music stops?" After hearing my diagnosis, I could not hear anything else but that word.

I knew that, if I was going to make it through this, I had to increase my faith. I knew that I had to give my faith some extreme Miracle-Gro. I sat back and thought about all the incomplete assignments and visions that God had given me. I knew that I could not have death as a mindset.

I started meditating on God and searching scriptures about healing. The particular scripture that I focused on was Ezekiel 37:4. It was when Ezekiel spoke to the dry bones. I read that scripture many times, but this particular time was different. I got a whole new revelation.

If dry bones can live by someone speaking to them, then I can speak to my pancreas to line up with the word of God. We must speak the word of God. I realized that every organ has ears. But, mainly healing has ears. We must speak it. We must speak to our victory. Victory is always there. Once victory hears our decree then it will rise up.

On the third day, I went to the Cleveland Clinic Cancer Center to set up my chemotherapy and radiation. I had made up my mind that I was going to go through whatever procedure needed for my long-life saving recovery. But I was going to come out with God by my side.

I sat there in the waiting room looking at the people around me. There were a lot of sick people in the waiting area and the lobby. When they called my name, it seemed as if I would never get to the examination room. I turned and waved at my family and friends. I become very silly when I am nervous, but the joy of the Lord had covered me. I encouraged my oldest daughter, Marquetta, who went to the examination room with me to remain joyful. I did not want anyone with me that was focused on death. If you were going to support me, you had to bring laughter, not sorrow.

Soon the intern came in and went over everything the doctors had shared with me. He talked about the liver and pancreatic cancer results. He went down his list of my symptoms and every answer was a *no*. The intern was in there close to an hour asking the same questions repeatedly while looking at his watch. "How long have you had stomach pain?" Can you keep anything down? Who do you live with?—and more. I got very anxious, I must say. So, I asked the Intern if my sister Detra could come to the room as well. We sat there another twenty minutes. My daughter and sister were not as patient as I was. So, the Intern finally left the room to see what was taking my physician so long.

After another ten minutes, my doctor finally came in. He talked about everything that they found on that Monday. He said that they carefully looked over test result again today. My doctor said, "Ms. Kelly, you do not have cancer." I honestly did not hear him. He said again, "Ms. Kelly, it is not cancer." All I could do was begin to praise God.

It was a minute before the doctor could complete what he was saying. The intern looked perplexed. I know that what they saw was cancer, but I know that God turned everything around! I was told that I had a non-cancerous tumor that only required one monthly injection. I said, Lord, I can deal with that! When I got back to the lobby, I tore it up with praise! We shouted, we praised, we worshipped, and we prayed for others in the lobby. It was an awesome time in the Lord. That increased my faith and showed God's glory! But this was just the beginning of another one of God's miracles in my life.

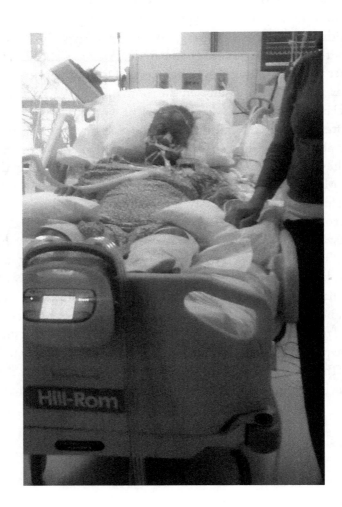

Am I Dreaming?

How do you share with someone that you have been to Heaven, yet you are still alive? Well, you don't look for a response from anyone. My Heaven experience began in December of 2016.

How do I tell you my experience? How can I tell others that I have been to Heaven?

My journey began with my dad. My daddy, "Mickey," was so handsome. He had a beautiful smile. I always wanted a special reltionship with him. Even though he was my step-dad, I always wanted to be close to him. I thought that if I was close to him, it would ruin my sister Lisa and his relationship. So, I held back the true love that I had for him until recently. He was a true man that cared about the health and wealth of his family. He was so dedicated to the family responsibility that he kept working. He was truly happy for my accomplishments. He wanted me to leave once I saw heaven. Dad told me that I would only be in Heaven a short time, but to be prepared for the places Dad would take me. I was prepared mentally, not phyically.

It was my Uncle Abraham's turn. He was my favorite uncle, and I was his favorite niece. He was a great giver. He was always giving something to somebody. Seeing him again was great for me because I truly missed him.

I saw my sister Gwen. I remember hugging her and waving goodbye just like I did the last time I saw her when she was living. It is nothing like a sister's love.

My dad wanted me to go to a nice formal event with him. So, I had to come home and get nice dress to wear. Before I got home, my cousin Joe had to give me a hug. Wow, it had been so many years since I saw him.

I wondered why my dad was always mistreated by people. I honestly think it was jealousy because he always worked hard for what he wanted and desired in life. He liked nice things, and he was determined to work to get those things. I don't know why he ended up in Cleveland. Yes, Uncle Abraham was there, but there had to be something that pushed Daddy to make a complete change by moving here. Whatever it was, it pushed my mom to move here too.

I also wondered why Daddy didn't go to church all the time (Lord knows we were there 24/7). But, it didn't stop him from knowing the history of God and the life of Jesus Christ. When it came close to his passing, he let us know that God was his Savior. I remember when he wanted to come to Affinity with me one Sunday. But Momma was not having that, so he went to her church, even though he actually loved Affinity.

Seeing that he was in heaven, that he loved the Lord, and that he was redeemed brought me so much joy.

There was no way that you could have told me I was in a coma. I remember seeing my sister Detra at her house and trying to find something to wear because, I was going somewhere with my dad. I was wondering why she would not talk to me. I thought it was because I was rambling in her clothes. That was the usual for me. I remember telling her that I would leave her alone, since she did not want to talk. She heard me moving, but she did not hear me speaking. I remember my daughter, Marquetta, being so busy, but I never saw where she was going. I was in a coma. She was so consumed with my health that she was basically there 24/7. Whatever issues I had with her growing up, we both loved each other. God answered her prayers. So, we can truly experience the love for each other.

ON THE OTHER SIDE

I literally thought I was dreaming, and it seemed to never end. That was not the case. So, now others will share their experience with what they witnessed.

Lisa Rush-(Baby Sister)

Are you not going to wake up? Please wake up! Wake up, wake up! This was my daily request to my sister...who laid lifeless in a coma. How could you not want to wake up? Eventually, you did, and it was at that moment I realized why you had chosen to sleep so long. Your first conversation after days, weeks of sleeping was a revelation that we as Christians only imagine once our time here is done. You spoke of visions both past and present, told us (Lisa, Detra, and Marquetta) that it was real, and if we wanted to go, we could.

The place you were referring to was Heaven. You tried to explain the colors that we have not yet seen but could only imagine. You spoke of the animals which have never walked on earth. Also, you saw our beloved Daddy, who had been our rock. The person who I occasionally got to see briefly in my dreams. His handsome loving face and quiet smile. Our sister Gwen that passed away, who every now and then waves to me from the back of a car, smiling and letting me know she is okay.

Dawn tried to explain the unlimited amount of food, but she only chose to eat salmon. She spoke of how our sister Detra would irritate her while she was in Glory. Me, with all that crying, Detra being on the cell phone, and the crying of our cousin Rennette, who lives miles away in Alabama.

Through your death experience, I was able to experience a closure of grief that held me for years. That, through hope, belief, and faith in Christ, we do live on when our natural bodies fail. Through my sister's tragedy, I was able to find peace again.

Detra Newton-(Big Sister)

On Sunday December 9th, 2016, what was normal for our family suddenly changed in the blink of an eye. Earlier, most of us attended church as we normally do, and, later that afternoon, my niece and I attended a chapter event, sponsored by my sorority, Zeta Phi Beta. Nevaeh did not want to go home, so I agreed to take her to school the next day if she spent the night with her grandmother. After an evening of relaxation, I sighed as I finally laid in bed with the anticipation of the next day being a busy work of day for me.

The phone rang and it was Nevaeh. She called and informed me that her grandmother was so sick and if I could come and see her. I thought it was my mother, as she had been ill lately. My niece went on to explain that it was not Grandma Wade, but Grandma Dawn.

I get up to put my clothes on, and the phone rang again. Now, she was crying and saying that her grandma passed out, and she asked if I could hurry. I immediately told her to hang up and call 911. I told her to leave the door cracked, and I was on my way. When I got there, Grandma Dawn was still out cold. So, I proceeded to remove her from the couch while talking to the EMS operator until the first response team arrived.

She was breathing, but shallowly. It was hard to get her awake. I continued to say her name to try to arouse her as I pleaded the blood of Jesus over her body. Having worked at healthcare for so long, I knew time was of the essence. It seemed like her body was lifeless.

The ambulance arrived, and she was transported to Cleveland Clinic hospital. Her daughter, Marquetta. met them there as I waited with our mother. My niece called shortly after and informed us that Grandma Dawn was hemorrhaging in her brain, and the doctors wanted her to sign paperwork for emergency surgery to relieve pressure. I began to pray, as I waited for my younger sister to arrive, so we could ride together.

Then...the storm...

When we got to the hospital, we were met with the news that we needed to call the family. We were given twenty-four hours, if that long.

What? How could this be? It took time to get myself together and when I did, I began to call my church family, friends, and my Sorors. We needed God to move in her life and move fast.

Well, He did, and the doctors were amazed at the thought that she was still with us. They felt that she would wake up in the next day or so after the anesthesia began to wear off. After staying at the hospital without leaving for three days, I felt comfortable to leave for just a few hours. I went into the room and whisper to Dawn that I was going to shower, check on our mother, and go to work for half a day, and I would see her when I returned. Out of nowhere, she spoke to me for the first time since Sunday. With her eyes still closed, she softly told me, "I won't be here." I then asked her jokingly, "Where are you going?"

She replied, "I will be in the upper room." It was 7:00 a.m.

By 9:00 a.m., she had suffered five seizures, and seizure number five took her almost to the point of no return. That night, I felt her in my house as she passed by me toward the door. This has not been the first time I experienced this. I felt something like this when our sister Gwen passed. She was in my house about a month before she went on. I shared with Pastor Maxwell and a few people what Dawn said and how I felt her spirit in my home. From the physical eye, you knew she was not there, and, from the spiritual eye, I knew that as well.

Days passed and turned to a week, and then about ten days later, the doctor told us that eventually we would have to make some hard decisions. She would probably decide for us, and there was nothing else they could do. One of the doctors, in his exact words, said, "I don't know why she wouldn't wake up. It's like when she tries to come back to, she would rescind back."

Well, for me it was confirmation of her spiritual journey and the decision that God would return her to us again. I felt a peace, because whatever happened now, I knew God was in control, and whatever his will was I would accept. To be absent from the body was to be present with the Lord. As Christians, this is often said, but do we really believe it?

Finally, on the twelfth day, she woke up and shared her spiritual journey with me, our younger sister Lisa, and her daughter Marquetta. Even now, she does not recall this conversation with the three of us, but we all were witnesses to her vision of the other side.

After her story was told, it also confirmed my faith that leaving this world is not an end, but a beginning. I must also include that, in giving her testimony, not once did she ever say that she was afraid. She said it was a beautiful place filled with joy. *Heaven is real!*

Nevaeh Kelly-(Granddaughter)

We never knew that something so small would be the biggest problem. This is how it all began. My grandmother was living with my great-grandmother, and I was staying there temporarily because she had recently had her foot amputated and needed help. My grandmother was going to work every day from 8:00 a.m. to 5:00 p.m., and sometimes she went earlier or had overtime. She had been complaining of a headache for the past few days, but she still wanted to do something for me for my birthday. My birthday was Thursday, December 8th, 2017.

On Saturday, December 10th, she threw me a hotel party. The entire party, my grandmother slept because her head was hurting. She had planned on going to church the next morning. She was dressed, but she didn't go. So later that day, she went to work, which was unusual because she doesn't work on weekends. She had to go to work because she had gotten an assignment on Friday a couple minutes before she left work that day, but the assignment was due Monday.

She got home at about 6:00 p.m. She was exhausted, and she usually goes to sleep late around 12:00 a.m. or 1:00 a.m. She went to sleep at nine, which was the same time I went to sleep. Before she fell asleep, she told me to put the trash can by her because she wasn't feeling good. We were both sleeping on the couches that were across from each other. She had started throwing up in her sleep, and I started panicking. Then I screamed her name constantly, with no response, so the first thing I did was run upstairs to get my great-grandmother.

I called 911, and then my great-grandmother called my auntie that lived in walking distance, only about three houses away. Once my auntie showed up, she was doing everything she could to wake my grandmother up, but she couldn't.

It took the ambulance forever to get there. By the time they got there, my auntie and uncle that lives in Bedford were there. I was extremely scared and crying, so I called my mom. My mom, dad, sister, and brother met the ambulance at the hospital. They had to pull the ambulance over on the side road and operate on her. Once they got to the hospital, they immediately put her on the ICU floor and put her in the coma. They gave her only twenty-four hours to live, but she made it. She had tubes in her head and everywhere else. She also had a ventilator to help her breathe.

She is truly a miracle. It took a lot of work, but she made it.

Marquetta Kelly-(Oldest Daughter)

Sometimes life will change right before your eyes. Isn't it amazing how that works? I am here to tell that, prior to this situation, my level of faith had declined very much. See, when God calls you to do his work and instills in you spiritual gifts that people pray a whole lifetime to receive and have yet failed to experience them, trust me, your faith is tested on a whole different level and scale. This may sound a little fishy to the non-believers, but this whole story is truly based on factual events. I couldn't make this up if I tried. My faith background is based on Pentecostal belief. I am a firm believer that Christ has walked on this earth, and while here he has delivered countless miracles that have led countless souls to God.

Even though I know who Jesus is, and I've seen his power too many times to question anything about my life, I'm only human. I was really questioning why my life was at a standstill. Everything was moving slowly for me. I had totally lost faith in my own life. I felt like there was no point of having faith in God, because he wasn't hearing me in the first place. Then, the day I woke up came.

It took place on a quiet Sunday winter night in December. We had just celebrated my eldest child Nevaeh's birthday earlier that day. My mom had been complaining of a headache the whole day and night. I had not thought nothing of it because we all suffer from migraines, so her having one wasn't out of the ordinary. Something was brewing inside my mommy's brain, and we didn't even know or see it coming.

She had been talking about attending church that morning. In fact, that's was her destination when we checked out the hotel that morning. Her and my daughter Nevaeh left to attend church and me and Heaven headed home. I had no clue that a few significant events were about to take place and test my faith even further.

My mom called me around five o'clock ranting and furious about the workload her job added to her long list of tasks she already had. How did she know this? Because she didn't go to church, she went to work instead and received an email that wasn't intended for her until Monday. So, not only was her head throbbing, but now her blood pressure was severely elevated I'm sure. Now, in addition to all that, she had to go care for my grandmother who had recently been discharged from rehabilitation for an amputation. I knew my mom was exhausted, but I just wasn't ready for the phone call I had just received. It was around 10:15 p.m. when my twelve-year-old called and told me that her grandmother wasn't responding, and she had called 911 and my aunt that stayed around the corner for help.

Everything for me at that moment went blank. I remember dressing my youngest two while talking on the phone with my oldest daughter. I told my fiancé, "We have to go now!"

We immediately left out the door. We decided to meet the ambulance at the hospital, since we had to pass the hospital to get to grandma's house. When we got there my mom's ambulance had not arrived yet. I couldn't even tell you how many times I was at that desk while calling to see if the ambulance had left. Only God can tell you how many conversations I had with him in my head before they arrived.

They walked us to the family room. I remember the seasoned doctor walking through the doors coming in the room where me, my fiancé, and two small children were placed. They were informing us that my mom had suffered an AVM, which mimics an aneurysm. It is a ball of blood vessels in her brain that ruptured, and she had been seizing non-stop since. Many people with this issue do not make it to the hospital and had a 1 percent survival rate. They told me her only chance would be the placement of tubes, and I had to sign the papers immediately. I was welcome to go see her.

As we walked to the room to see her, I literally felt like I was taking a walk into twilight city. When I got back there, it was like a piece a me couldn't contain myself. She was there naked and convulsing non-stop with her eyes just rolling.

At that time, I was very scared. It was so unbelievable. I remembered calling my aunt's phone and losing my mind while pacing back and forth. The medical team had decided to take her to the neuro ICU for observation for twenty-four hours. That was the approximate time that they had given her to live.

Me, my fiancé, kids, aunts, and uncle waited in that waiting room for six hours before anyone came in and said anything. We were beyond scared. I did not realize that my faith at the that exact moment had no choice but to be restored. Things were so unstable, and the doctors didn't have much of anything to say to us. They told us that, if she woke up, it was more than likely she would be in a vegetable state with left-side weakness and many other injuries. As I stated it was a big *if*.

My whole family was going though it with numerous people at the hospital everyday expecting a prognosis. Man, things were really getting crazy, and I was the biggest mess there was. Refusing to eat, sleep, or think, I was at a standstill. Then one day, I knew God was telling me to play gospel music for my mother to hear. I was playing that music and singing to her, hoping that she could hear. I believe it was that Tuesday when they tried to wake her up and she woke, but instantly started having seizures. While awake, she told my aunt that she was going to the upper room.

My aunt, thinking nothing of it, had to go back to work. Maybe fifteen minutes later, I arrived back to the hospital. That quickly, my mother had to be put back in the coma. It appeared that everything was turning for the worse, but I kept praying, and I kept worshipping, and I kept asking God to do His will no matter what. I recall sitting on the toilet later that night, bawling out to God, and I just heard my mother voice tell me to "Put the big girl panties on," which was her favorite little saying. I had thought nothing of it until my aunt called me and said that she had felt my mother spirit in her house. In fact, she had stopped going home if she was alone. What a coincidence, and for us to think we were losing our minds.

This went on for days, and days turned into weeks. To the natural eye, all hope was leaving quickly because, not only was she in a coma, she was very, very ill as well. She was on a ventilator on a chilled bed with an inflatable heating blanket with an elevated temperature and elevated blood pressure. She was going through some things outside of her body, and we had no idea what was going on.

Let me be very truthful in telling you that I had really started losing faith. Things were not moving fast enough for my faith level. I needed things to turn around and turn around very quickly before I really lost it. It's amazing that when bad arises, people come out the woodwork. All the phone calls and texts we received were overwhelming. It was really a lot to take in. We never really had an update for them, but they were appreciated at the same time.

It had come to the point where they had to unhook the ventilator, and we needed God to perform a miracle like never before. This was just unbelievable. People suggested that I call the funeral home. It felt like *The Twilight Zone*. Family and friends' comprehension at a zero, not understanding how big of responsibility was being put on my shoulders. With my sister at school in Michigan, my shoulders felt quite heavy. I prayed and prayed and prayed. My prayer was, "Lord have Your way, not my way, but Yours." I remember walking in my mother's hospital room and saying, "Today is the day they said they have to unplug you, that you need to hurry up and decide if you are going to stay in Heaven or come back." I told her that no matter what she decided, I would be okay with it (even though that part was lie). When they took her off the ventilator, all her body functions kicked in perfectly.

The same body functions that were elevated, the same body functions that were the secondary reason that almost took her life. I remember them putting her in a jerry chair and wheeling her downstairs to see the Christmas tree. I remember her memory being a little foggy. I remember her asking for my papa non-stop, who had passed four years prior.

She just kept telling me and my aunts the story of Michael Jackson taking her around the city in a chariot and she had a big beautiful gown on. The streets were made of gold. She said she enjoyed a beautiful ball and ate salmon. As a matter of fact, it took several weeks after her awaking to believe that Papa had died because she had just spent so much time with him. For those of you who for some strange reason do not believe in the power of God, I am here to tell you that its very real and He is still performing miracles daily.

Eugene Lott-(Ex-Son in Law)

I had just seen her the morning before she got in the coma. I was picking my wife and youngest daughter up from the hotel where my oldest daughter had her sleepover. I remember pretending to hit her with the car, and she said, "Boy, stop playing." We left and went our separate directions and that was that.

My older daughter stayed with her grandma. Later that night, while my wife and I were in the bed, we received a phone call from Nevaeh saying that her grandma was throwing up and wasn't breathing. My wife started putting the babies' coats on, and we ran out the house to get to the hospital. The doctors came in with bad news saying that she had 24 hours to live. My wife was breaking down. It was just so unbelievable, but it did not hit until we saw her. It was crazy.

Our babies were right there with us, and everyone was distraught. All I could do was be a support system for my wife, while not knowing the outcome. A couple weeks had went passed, and it didn't seem like things were getting any better. I remember going back there telling Dawn that, if she woke up, I would cut my dreads off since she liked seeing me with my short haircut. Needless to say, I have a bag full of dreads in the bottom of my closet.

Linda Belcher-(Spiritual Sister)

Viewing Dawn's journey from Heaven and back from the opposite side of Earth. It was a Monday morning, approximately 9:22 a.m., when I received a call from her eldest daughter as her journey had begun the night before.

Tay's voice beckoned in my ear stating, "My mom is not doing too good." I immediately requested her to repeat what she said as I was having the hardest time comprehending her response. The telephone had seemed to quiet down and fall back into the background sound of my echoing tears bellowing from the pit of my gut. Anyone who loves someone would not want to hear their loved one is not doing well. I did not how to feel but afraid, lonely, and numb while my best-friend was lying between the thresholds of life and death's door. I continued to cry uncontrollably, pleading with God and reminding Him of what He had said and promised her. Her work was not yet done!

I rushed to the hospital to wait patiently in family lounge with Dawn's family and close friends. No one knew what to expect, instead just waiting to hear good news. We reminisced and exchanged stories to pass time along as we were awaiting change for the better and an awaking from her extended sleep. Dawn was in a coma in response to an Arteriovenous Malformation Rupture in her brain, and the doctors had no clear understanding and greatly questioned how she medically survived such a traumatic brain injury. The day had grown late in the afternoon once we were able to finally visit her in the ICU. To my surprise, my best-friend was lying in bed with several tubes and medical devices hooked to her weakened body—from her skull to her feet. I asked myself, *Who is this?*

I was not mentally or spiritually prepared for what I saw. There was a tube inserted through her cranial bone into her brain to drain the overflow of blood in her brain into a bag hanging on an IV pole next to her. Silently I began to cry again, and I heard the Lord say, "No," very loudly. I was not sure what that "No" meant, and, at the time, nothing made sense. My faith was shaken, and I was a little angry with God as I stood there asking Him why He had taken my friend from me while she was still present, however not able to respond.

The following day, at about 5:30 p.m., I was getting dressed to go back to the hospital to visit Dawn. While in my upstairs bathroom, I turned on the water to brush my teeth when I suddenly heard a voice. It was Dawn's voice. She instructed me to look after her eldest daughter. I quickly started flushing the toilet and turning the faucet water to full blast trying to drown out the voice. I truly thought it was my imagination until I felt a touch as I looked around to see no one was there.

Trusting God in all of this, I continued to the hospital. Once I arrived, several visitors were rallying in the halls and the adjacent family lounge. Shortly after my arrival, everyone began to retire and go home. Her daughter, Marquetta, and I sat in the lounge waiting to go back to Dawn's room. I knew then that the voice I had heard was indeed Dawn's. Her daughter Tay was strong and faced shadows with remnants of worry and fear, asking if she is doing the right things for her mother.

As days passed, everyone began to hold strongly onto their faith. However, many felt some fear. I know fear and faith cannot walk hand and hand. There were so many emotions. I realized one night, while sitting with Dawn and her daughter Tay, there was a purpose for what Dawn was going through. Embracing the purpose was all we had.

We began laughing, joking, singing and playing gospel music. We were doing what we would do if Dawn was able to join in with us. Funny to say, we even made jokes about her, saying, "She is probably going over her contract and negotiating in Heaven." Some may think that is crazy, however it really wasn't.

At about 10:30 p.m. that night, I noticed Dawn's expressions was changing. There were no significant psychical changes—it appeared spiritual. It looked as if Dawn was transitioning from her body going from place to place, and then she would return. At times, she looked empty; I would look at her again, and she looked like she was full of life and was just sleeping. I began to have hope that one day I would be able to have a conversation with her again.

God has a funny way of getting our attention. I embraced the transitioning as well as those who God had trusted with this. The feeling of apprehension and being afraid of losing my friend was still in the back of my mind. However, I vowed to hang in there with her daughters, sisters, mom, and family.

The "No" I heard from God had become very apparent as to why He said no. The Lord had brought a number of people together because of Dawn's condition. I felt I had to protect her while not knowing she was actually protecting us. It makes me wonder why one seems to be the big example of sacrifice for the purpose of others. We were created in God's image and supposed to be like Christ. Through Dawn's AVM rupture, there was a change in my life. My perspective on life is different, and I had begun evaluating my life, learning to be assertive, and ridding myself of worries. The time she was in the coma briefly, I was selfishly upset I could not have a conversation with her. I had to stand by and truly wait to hear from God. He said I must trust in Him totally and to have no doubt.

There was scare upon scare as the doctors began to notice Dawn's condition looked to worsen before it had gotten better. Doctors are often given a bad reputation by being accused of not being spiritually in tune. We have to remember being a child of God is not limited to a certain group or population of people. Dawn's doctors were spiritually aware of her transitioning. We had continued to pray. I prayed, asking God to show us some sign of brain activity. The doctors were not sure if she would be brain dead or even have any productive brain activity without having a seizure in the process. The doctor had begun to monitor for brain activity placing leads all over her scalp.

A couple nights later, while sitting with her eldest daughter in the ICU, something remarkable had occurred. We began to listen to recorded sermons online and pray. Shortly, we started playing worship music and laid the cell phone near for Dawn to hear. The respiratory nurses had come in to check and monitor her breathing while she was on the respirator. Before exiting the room, the nurse gave us a few encouraging words and told us a story about her mother.

We continued to sit while singing along with the music. Briefly, I take a glance at her electroencephalogram (EEG), noticing repetitive movement. Not having understanding for what each reading indicated, the Lord made provision for us to see brain activity. Dawn was able to hear us! Her blood pressure began to briefly elevate during powerful strong melodies in the songs. The auditory lead reading reflected beautiful rhythmic patterns to every note and every word. Dawn heard the worship music. That was truly a praise report. The following week, I received a call from her daughter only to surprisingly hear Dawn's faint voice.

Dawn's journey continued during recovery from her AVM. She was cognitively impaired, briefly having difficulty putting her thoughts together after days and weeks of coming out of her coma. Dawn described Heaven in vivid detail, and she even reassured us by the telling everyone Heaven was definitely real.

When I saw her for the first time post-coma, she recognized me and a few others. Dawn had such a peace and glow upon her that I had never seen before on anyone. She recalled some of the laughter and conversation we had while she was in the coma. After the coma, everyone that came into her presence was infected with her joy and her love from God. She could not remember much prior to her injury immediately. The doctors could not understand or knew what to expect. *It was a miracle from Heaven.*

Aretha Young-(Sweet Big Sister)

While preparing myself to be with my sister Dawn and not knowing what to expect, I was very upset and sad. When I made it to Cleveland traveling from Mississippi, I entered her hospital room with tears in my eyes. When she saw my face she said, "Girl what are you crying for? I'm okay! I'm alive, and I got a story to tell!"

I said, "Well, go on and tell it!"

Alvin Frazier-(Close Friend)

The morning of December 12th, 2016, I woke up to a notification on Facebook in my inbox from an old high school friend telling me to call him and that it was important. I called, and he went on to tell me that our mutual friend Dawn had suffered an aneurysm, or so we thought, and had become comatose.

I was worried and very concerned for my friend. After hearing the details of what happened, I sat there sort of numb and wondered, *How could this be?* Remembering a recent text conversation she and I had a couple days earlier, what came to mind was how stressed out she said she was and how the tone of her message seemed a bit agitated.

Dawn and I had been friends for over ten years and had become like family. I had recently moved away to NYC, so the crew consisting of Dawn, Terri, Cheryl and myself would try to get together whenever I was in town. Dawn had become very busy lately with work, so we weren't able to catch up as usual. She sent me a long text message expressing how sorry she was for having to cancel or reschedule our outings during that trip home. Of course, I understood and assured her there were no worries, but I recalled that she seemed overwhelmed from all she had going on at the time, especially with her job. I had no idea that later on that evening we would almost lose her.

When I arrived at Cleveland Clinic a few days later, I honestly didn't know what to expect. After taking a few deep breaths, I proceeded into the hospital and hoped for the best. The waiting room was filled with family and friends. I immediately recognized Dawn's sisters and eldest daughter. We greeted one another, and they explained the details of Dawn's condition. Apparently, she was responsive but heavily sedated and not in the best of moods, so the hospital staff wouldn't allow anyone to visit her most of the day until that evening.

Finally, they permitted visitors two at a time, and, being as close as I am to Dawn, I was allowed to go in after family. Seeing her in the condition she was in was hard to process initially, but somehow, I knew she would make a full recovery. I truly believed that, but the question was when?

The next few weeks were very touch and go. I saw Dawn's strength so many times during that period, and I was so proud of her. There were good days when she was alert, and others where she was non- responsive. Days where she responded well to the memory and recognition tests, and others when she was very disoriented and confused. For me, the bad days were the hardest because I wanted so badly for her to be okay, and I knew she was really trying to be.

Witnessing her turnaround from the state she was in when she arrived to when she was released was a true testament of God's power, purpose, and plan for Dawn's life going forward. She was on a mission before but now it was even more clear and evident that her assignment was not complete. It was only getting started...

Rev. William Howard Kelly, Jr.-(Brother)

I saw Dawn lying in a state of non-responsiveness. I actually thought she was going to die. Then I remembered that she and I are children of God. My faith kicked in. As I begin to pray, I knew that Dawn would live and as they say the rest is history. God is _awesome_.

Willie Bell Wade-(Mother)

Dawn went into a deep sleep, and no one could wake her up or bring her back but God. God showed her some things that only he could do. God gave her a chance to tell her story in a book. So, that anyone who reads it, will be touched by the words. In Joel 2:28 (NIV), it says, "And it shall come to pass afterward, that I will pour out my spirit upon all flesh; and your sons and your daughters shall prophesy, your old men shall dream dreams, your young men shall see visions."

<u>Terrence Rush-(Brother in Law)</u>

If you never knew about God's love, grace, and mercy or have seen a miracle just a few months ago as I witnessed all the above by God showing me through the miraculous recovery of Dawn Kelly's life experience of death and being brought back to live again on this earth, all I can say is, *Wow.* The doctors said this was it; however, God had the last word, and he said this wasn't!

Lideja C. White-(Baby Daughter)

When I got that call from Marquetta that you were on your way to the hospital, everything around seemed to stop! My mother is my world, and honestly, I would not know what to do without her. Me living in another state was already a lot for me, especially not being able to get there in a hurry.

When I got the news about my mother's condition, I just started praying. I never thought that this would happen to my mother My mom is a strong, independent, God-fearing woman. Going through these trials and tribulations made me closer to God. It made me appreciate life and everyone around me.

GOD IS SO AWESOME!

I had experienced so many miracles by God. My mom was told that I would be aborted because she had an emergency appendicitis surgery while pregnant with me. I have survived so many health issues—the measles, the mumps, tonsillitis, I almost went blind because of a small drop of perm in my eyebrow, and I threw up blood as a child and they could not find where it was coming from. I had cellulitis twice. The first time almost took me out of here. I had to have a hysterectomy, but I had to receive several blood transfusions before it could be done. After it was done the following day, I had to have an emergency surgery because my stomach had filled with blood, and they could not find out where it was coming from. All they could do was clean the blood out of my stomach. They still don't know where it came from.

I was hit in three car accidents in a year and a half (not one was my fault). The last one sent me in the air, and I hit a pole on the opposite side and a distance from where I was hit. It goes on and on. To be in a coma, but in Heaven was a miracle of all miracles. I always knew I was called by God. I never thought I was better than anyone, but somehow some people thought I was being phony. They were jealous of me when I never believed in myself. I had visions and wrote each one of them down. Every time I attempted to complete them, I would get distracted by an illness.

So, I began to think that not one of my visions would be fulfilled. I have always encouraged others that looked troubled, but I dealt with my troubles by praying and not allowing my troubles to get me in a depressed state of mind. I have gotten accused, talked about, lied to, and definitely mistreated. Even still, I still treated those people with respect as much as I could. The sad thing is that the people who do the most hurt to others are Christians. Many pastors, preachers, apostles, and so on treat people like they are higher and greater than God. If we were perfect, then we would not need God.

There is no one, not one that does and lives a completely perfect life. Some Christians won't even say hello to the homeless because they are dirty or smell. They are more focused on themselves. How can you expect a great congregation when you are too good to shake their hands? I thank God for my church, Affinity Missionary Baptist Church. I had to leave a few times, but they were assignments from God. It had nothing to do with the church. It had nothing to do with my pastor, Pastor Maxwell.

Now, please do not get it confused. I am not Baptist. I am not Catholic. I am not Holiness, or Protestant. What and who I am is a child of God. Saved, but only by God's grace. He knows each and every mistake that I would make before I made them. I just pray that the pastors that are putting themselves in front of God would stop. Please! It grieves the Holy Spirit. The last church that God called me for a mission was not pleasing to God. I loved the Pastor and knew her before I even joined, but I pray for her because I know she is anointed. But she must obey God.

Everyone that walked with Jesus was far from perfect. They had all kinds of major issues, but he allowed them to do that because that was an awesome way to change them. Some did change and some didn't, but Jesus knew before it even happened. What we must realize is that God knows and sees everything. We need to be honest with others, but especially with God! He has brought all of us out of so many things, whether we believe it or not.

I don't know about anyone else that has a relationship with God and hears the things that he may direct you to go or do, but my heart weighs heavy when God directs me to do or say something that needs to be said. There are too many Christian leaders that do not know how to minister and love. But, enough of that. That will be my next book.

Well, I had a test that no one wanted me to have. Family was just grateful that I was alive, but I know God is greater. Honestly, I have not met anyone with my faith. I know that someone exists, but not in my family or any of my friends. On November 22nd, I had to receive a Gamma Knife test which involved a lot of X-rays, CT scans, and the last test was the one-time radiation on my brain where the AVM burst. These were all done in one day. I had to take all these procedures in a crown that looked something like what they put on Jesus' head when they nailed him to the cross. Even though mine was very heavy metal, I am sure it did not feel even close to what Jesus suffered for us.

The radiation took fifty minutes to finish. After it was over and the plate was removed, my head was in the worst pain I have ever felt. They would not release me to leave until an hour after removing it. I was in a lot of pain, but I kept thinking about Jesus. I had a little bleeding, but I was a little better the next day. The results from the radiation would take at least a year to receive. Before the radiation, my doctor came in and told me that there were no tangled veins anymore, just a small cyst. *Praise God again!* He just keeps doing miracles!

Yesterday I received the results on the website that I can check. It stated that *everything* was normal! I had gone through another miracle! God put His miraculous touch on my brain, and He repaired it! Have you ever heard of a marvelous 2017 thing? If you doubt God, you better increase your faith! Stop looking at finances, issues, doubters, haters, what you lack, and what others have, other people's relationships, the fact that you are single, the fact that you have children out of wedlock, the fact that you didn't graduate from high school, and the fact that you are not the place in life where you feel you should be. You are still alive! God is still with you! He still cares! So, keep moving, never give up, and never let anyone that lacks their self-esteem prey on yours.

I have several close friends that it was too many, it would be too long to get this book out. I know that there is someone that needs to hear my story. I was only supposed to be a vegetable if I survived. But, look at My God! I am not 100 percent, but as Oprah Winfrey said in

The Color Purple, "I am still here!"

I still have a long road of healing to travel, but let me tell you, I know now that now my ministry will be effective because God did the miraculous not only in my life, but in those around me. So, I say today to believe God, trust God, and know that He can do anything. There is nothing too difficult for Him to do. There is *not one thing!* Increase your faith, and God will show you His Glory!

LORD,

I WILL NEVER FORGET ALL THE

MIRACULOUS

AND

WONDERFUL THINGS YOU HAVE DONE FOR

ME!

3/6/1969-8/14/2019
Lisa Wade-Rush

CPSIA information can be obtained
at www.ICGtesting.com
Printed in the USA
BVHW041601021220
594663BV00013B/75